D1199539

Library of Congress Cataloging-in-Publication Data
Thomson, Ruth.
All About Shapes.

(My first easy and fun books)
Bibliography: p.
Summary: Presto the magician performs a number of tricks with circles, triangles, and other shapes.
[1. Shape--Fiction. 2. Magicians--Fiction] I. Ives, Penny, ill. II. Title. III. Series: Thomas, Ruth. My first easy and fun
books.
PZ7.T38Sh   1987   [E]   87-42587
ISBN 1-55532-339-1
ISBN 1-55532-314-6 (lib. bdg.)

North American edition first published in 1987 by
Gareth Stevens, Inc.
7221 West Green Tree Road Milwaukee, WI 53223, USA

Original text copyright © 1986 by Ruth Thomson.
Supplementary text copyright © 1987 by Gareth Stevens, Inc.
Illustrations copyright © 1986 by Penny Ives.

First published as *Shapes* in the United Kingdom by Walker Books Ltd.

Typeset by Web Tech, Inc., Milwaukee. Printed in Italy.
Series Editor: MaryLee Knowlton.

1 2 3 4 5 6 7 8 9 92 91 90 89 88 87

MY FIRST EASY AND FUN BOOKS

ALL ABOUT

shapes

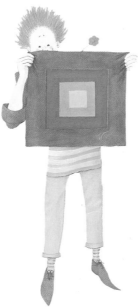

By Ruth Thomson
Illustrated by Penny Ives

Gareth Stevens Publishing
Milwaukee

Good afternoon, boys and girls! I am
Presto, the world-famous magician.

Do you want to see my very
best tricks? Yes? Then let's begin!

square

First I take a big, **square** hanky.

I crumple it up. Abracadabra!

Presto! Not one, not two, not three, but four **square** hankies!

circle

Now watch. I have three **circles.**
I have string tied to my wrists.

Presto! The **circles** are on the string.

triangle

Count the **triangles** on my flag.

The flag goes into my hat. Tap, tap!

Presto! A whole row of flags.
How many **triangles** are there now?

rectangle

What a picture!
It's a big **rectangle**.

I cut it into little
rectangles.

I put the **rectangles**
into a bag.

Presto! A whole
picture again.

diamond

See the **diamond** shapes on my cloth.

I shake the cloth. Abracadabra!

Presto! The cloth is plain and the **diamond** shapes are in my hand!

cone

Look! I have three **cones**, all the same. I put an egg under one **cone**.

I shuffle the **cones** around.
Presto! A fluffy chick!

cube

This is my magic **cube.**

Anything inside it? No.

But presto! There's another **cube** inside and a rabbit inside that!

sphere

Three balls go into my hat. They are called **spheres**. Abracadabra!

Presto! Look how the balls have changed! But they are still **spheres.**

cylinder

Here is an empty **cylinder.**

It <u>is</u> empty, isn't it?

I say the magic word, and presto! I have made myself a delicious drink.

That's the end of my show, boys and girls. Did you enjoy it?

Before you go, play my special game.
What shapes can you see on the stage?

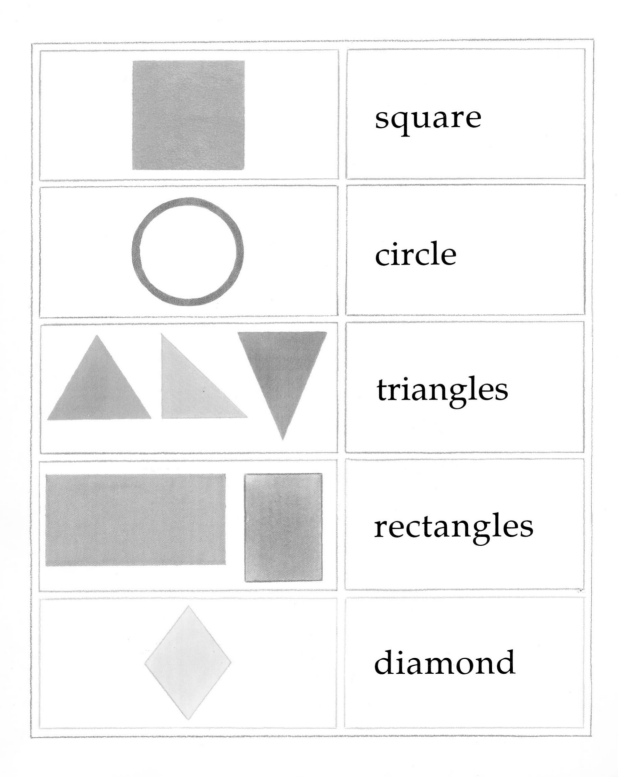

square

circle

triangles

rectangles

diamond

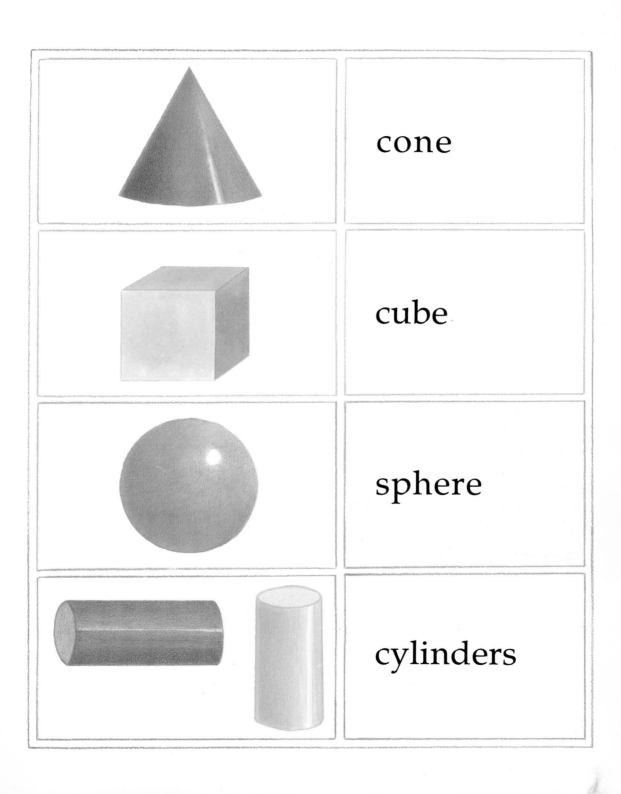

cone

cube

sphere

cylinders

Things To Do

1. Name the shapes of foods in your refrigerator.

2. Watch the clouds. Can you see shapes or objects in them?

3. Look through magazines or catalogs for pictures that are shapes. Cut them out and paste them on paper to make a shape book of your own.

4. Look for shapes! Take a walk. Look for shapes in buildings. Find triangles, circles, squares, and rectangles. What shapes do you find most often?

5. Take a walk around your house with a piece of paper and a pencil. On the piece of paper, make four columns. At the top of each, write a shape. Look for things of that shape and write them in the proper column. You can do this with friends, too, and see who gets the longest lists.

More Books About Shapes

Care Bears' Circus of Shapes. Kahn (Random House)

Get Ready: Colors and Shapes. Muntean (Random House/Children's Television Workshop)

Is It Larger? Is It Smaller? Hoban (Greenwillow)

Old Hat, New Hat. Berenstain (Random House)

The Shape of Me and Other Stuff. Dr. Seuss
    (Random House)

Shapes. Pienkowski (Little Simon)

Shapes. Reiss (Aladdin)

Shapes. Satchwell (Random House)

Stencil Book of Objects. Tallarico (Tuffy
    Learning Books)